OliviaNewton-John

text   **Ann Morse**
illustrations   **John Keely**
design concept   **Mark Landkamer**

published by   **Creative Education**
    Mankato, Minnesota

Published by Creative Educational Society, Inc.,
123 South Broad Street, Mankato, Minnesota 56001
Copyright © 1976 by Creative Educational Society, Inc. International
copyrights reserved in all countries.
No part of this book may be reproduced in any form without written
permission from the publisher. Printed in the United States.
Distributed by Childrens Press,
1224 West Van Buren Street, Chicago, Illinois 60607

Library of Congress Numbers: 75-25849   ISBN 0-87191-475-1

Library of Congress Cataloging in Publication Data
Morse, Ann.   Olivia Newton-John
1. Newton-John, Olivia—Juvenile literature.
I. Keely, John.   II. Title.
ML3930.N495M6   784'.092'4(B)   75-25849   ISBN 0-87191-475-1

Pure and Simple

It was almost as though the moment were made for her singing—a moment pure and simple—like the song she was singing, "I Honestly Love You." She stood poised and straight in a very green garden. Trees hung in clumps over her head. Her light blue, pleated, chiffon dress cast an almost mystical aura about her. Though everything about her was simple and understated, the moment was charged with energy and release. "But this is pure and simple and you must realize that / It's comin' from my heart and not my head." Without a gesture, Olivia Newton-John pushed her listeners over the edge, onto a plane of pure feeling.

Olivia's part in Paul Williams' TV special, *Listen, That's Love,* was a performance complete in itself; but it was more than that. It was part of a fuller experience Paul Williams offered TV audiences that evening in late spring, 1975.

Paul and his guests—Olivia, Helen Reddy, Rosalind Kind, and Seals & Crofts — communicated a personal concept about the beauty of love — a beauty that was tapped perhaps only through musical expression. Olivia sang only one song on the show. Yet her presence remained. Along with the other singers, she had expressed the kind of warmth the world can't really do without.

"If Not For You"

"If Not For You" was Olivia's real beginning. Dylan wrote the song in 1970 and Olivia recorded it in 1971. It is light and catchy with an easy flow. And Olivia knew how to change it — just enough to make it into her own sound. She changed a few verses, dropping words at the end of phrases. Instead of tacking on lines like, "And you know it's true," and "Oh, what would I do," Olivia simply let her voice drift. The melody is definite and Olivia sang it simply.

7

Dylan's version is written for acoustic guitar and harmonica accompaniment. In Olivia's recording, the acoustic guitar maintains the beat while the steel pedal guitar provides a kind of echo. (A steel guitar is an electrified pedal instrument with a zither-like set of strings.) When Dylan calls for a harmonica solo, Olivia calls for an electric guitar solo. The effect is a country sound and a strange combination of softness and strength.

Olivia made "If Not For You" as a single recording for Festival Records International in England. It became a hit in the United Kingdom, Australia, South Africa, and Belgium — and, as *Billboard* reported, it became number 1 in Italy. Its rise to popularity in the United States was more gradual. Olivia had to perform more before many Americans would begin to take notice of her.

Growing Up with Music

Olivia Newton-John was born in October, 1948, in Cambridge, a sparsely populated city just north of London, England. Cambridge is in low-lying country with dikes and canals, making it look like Holland. Cambridge, less modernized than most of England's cities, is most famous for its renowned Cambridge University. The University campus is a myriad of spires and stained glass, buildings that exude medieval splendor. Olivia's parents found Cambridge an invigorating, stimulating place in which to live and work.

Olivia's mother was born in Germany and was well educated. She received some notoriety as the daughter of a Nobel prize-winning physicist, Max Born. Olivia's

Welsh-born father was a professor of German at Cambridge. When Olivia was five, her father was named Master of Ormond College at the University of Melbourne — so Mr. and Mrs. Newton-John took Olivia and her older brother and sister to Australia. Later, Olivia's parents were divorced.

For the next eleven years, Australia was Olivia's home. A dry, flat and ancient land mass, Australia is washed by three oceans. It is a land of contrasts — green rolling plains and blazing red ranges, dense jungles and thousands of miles of monotonous desert. The row of highlands flanking the eastern coast shelters the big cities and the lush farms of Australia's most resourceful section. Olivia and her family lived in this eastern part, in the city of Melbourne.

Melbourne is the capital of Victoria which is often called the luckiest state in Australia. It has almost none of the wasteland that spreads across many of the five other Australian states. In contrast to the other states, Victoria is a rich combination of city, bush and farm, mountains, plains and valleys. Its rural areas contain rich dairy pasture and fertile mountain valleys. Its cities are near the sea and so become ports for industry.

The Newton-Johns moved to Melbourne in the early 1950's when factories began springing up and the city began to grow rapidly. Though the city's population is over 3 million, Melbourne has always reflected a kind of quiet dignity. Olivia's family would stroll down Melbourne's wide, tree-lined streets. They'd watch the trams trundle on old grid patterns in the street and stop at the botanical gardens in the city's square.

Olivia became used to a hazy blue presence in Melbourne's eastern sky — the Dandenong Ranges. So, while the Newton-Johns lived in a metropolitan area, they were always surrounded by natural beauty. The city and its mountains left an impact on young Olivia.

In a nearby park, Healsville sanctuary, it was not unusual for Olivia and her brother and sister to see kangaroos, platypuses, koala bears and wombats. Olivia has always admitted to an intense fascination in animals. The parks provided a kind of gentle serenity for Olivia; the mountains assured adventure.

Also, Melbourne has thrived on sporting and cultural events. Two of Olivia's favorite pastimes — playing tennis and riding horses — reflect major interests in Melbourne. Australia has become known as the birthplace of some of the finest professional tennis players in the world. Like Olivia, almost everyone learns the game at a young age. But horses have become just as important as tennis. Melbourne is the only city in the world which annually takes a day off for a horse race. Every year the Newton-Johns would join in the festivities surrounding the Melbourne Cup Classic at Flemington. The race was held on the first Tuesday of November, and the whole nation would stop to listen to the race broadcast.

Music concerts also colored the Newton-John's calendar. Olivia's father had long struggled with the idea of becoming an opera singer before he chose a teaching career. Olivia shared her father's interest in music. At five, she was already picking out songs on the family piano. She would spend hours amusing her sister and friends with her made-up songs. Her family recognized her musical interest and encouraged her singing and songwriting.

Her father had a collection of a thousand records, mostly classical. "But he gave me Tennessee Ernie Ford records, too," Olivia says. Other musical people who caught Olivia's ear when she was young were Ray Charles, Joan Baez and Nina Simone. "Music is just in the Welsh blood," Olivia said, "and it was with me through my childhood."

At eight, Olivia was fascinated by Slim Dusty's music. Slim Dusty, the dean of country music in Australia, has spent most of his life turning the folklore of his country's "outback" into song. He and his fellow-traveling entertainers would take their country shows throughout the inland areas of Australia, often where no roads existed. Olivia listened to Slim's recordings on the radio and heard the tales of his travels. Olivia now calls Dusty's music her first introduction to country music.

When Olivia was fourteen, she and three friends needed something to do; so they formed a singing group called "The Sol Four." They had fun getting together for practice and singing at school and small community gatherings. They even landed a few spots on local TV. The four girls were enjoying their singing so much that schoolwork became almost a pastime. Olivia's parents and the other girls' parents objected, and the group disbanded.

The breakup of "The Sol Four" didn't stop Olivia's singing, however. When her brother-in-law suggested she sing at his coffee lounge, Olivia jumped at the chance. She immediately felt at ease performing. It was almost as if the fast tempo of Melbourne and the easy pace of the countryside had crept into her blood. Even at 15, Olivia filled her performances with remarkable variety. Her audiences sensed it, too, and appreciated her flowing manner. Audience reaction greatly encouraged Olivia and increased her self-confidence.

It was a customer at the coffee lounge who gave her

an idea which eventually launched her career. He suggested that Olivia enter a talent contest organized by
Johnny O'Keefe, a popular Australian record and TV artist.

To no one's surprise, Olivia won the contest. The
prize entitled her to a boat trip to London. But Olivia's
mother felt she should stay in school another year. Olivia
stayed; but at 16, she felt she had to make a decision. She
had to choose between finishing her last year in school or
going on to seek stardom. She chose stardom.

Remembering her famous grandfather, Max Born,
who was Albert Einstein's best friend, Olivia looked back
on her decision saying, ". . . and look what happened to
me? Two plus two is five." At 16, Olivia was like a branch
breaking away from the family's tree in the academic world
— not an easy thing for a teen-ager to do. She felt
somewhat relieved that her older brother had done what
many in the family had wanted — he had gone through
extensive schooling and became a brilliant doctor. Olivia's
sister, however, helped to pave the way for the young
singer. At 15, the older daughter had left school to become
an actress. It wasn't such a shock, then, when Olivia
sailed for her homeland, England, hoping to become a
singing star.

The late 1960's in England provided stimulating
musical experiences for Olivia. But she seemed to crawl
toward stardom at a snail's pace. At first, Olivia tasted
London's music market with *Tomorrow,* a teenybop
group.

Not long after Olivia tired of the teen group, she
teamed up with another Australian girl, Pat Carroll. The
two Aussie singers scheduled BBC television shows and
some cabaret performances. The girls had a chance to try
out different styles and test their sound, but usually Olivia's

easy manner prevailed. By 1970, Olivia and Pat were meeting new people and making contacts in music circles.

It was then that Olivia met Cliff Richard, one of England's most famous rock stars. In 1958, before the Beatles, Cliff Richard began his career with a hit, "Move It," which made him England's "Elvis." Richard continued singing smooth, "unheavy" songs. He appeared on TV, made films, and toured every year. For over fifteen years, Cliff Richard has been popular with the English.

After Pat Carroll's visa ran out in 1971 and she was forced to return to Australia, Olivia began touring with Cliff Richard and his troop. As a solo performer, Olivia watched Richard and learned much from him. She studied how he put a show together, and she observed the ease with which he sang soft rock songs. Being a newcomer to touring, Olivia usually had to be the first act of a show. The warm-up spot on a show is always difficult because the audience is waiting for the bigger star. But watching the others perform, Olivia used the opportunity to learn more about performing.

Traveling with Cliff Richard brought additional contacts. Frequently, *The Shadows* played backup for Cliff. The group eventually disbanded. But Bruce Welch, John Farrar and John Rostill of *The Shadows* would later write and arrange songs for Olivia. In fact, Rostill wrote two of Olivia's biggest hits, "Let Me Be There" and "If You Love Me, Let Me Know." John Farrar wrote "Have You Never Been Mellow?".

Early in 1971, Olivia recorded her first single for Festival Records International, "If Not For You." It became a hit all over Europe. An album by the same name followed but generated little interest. Then Olivia's name surfaced again with another successful single, "Banks of the Ohio."

14

Her initial outing, "If Not For You," made a heavy chart dent in *Billboard's* "Hot 100 and Top 40 Easy Listening." Follow-up folk rock ballad offers same potency.

"Top 60 Spotlight"
Billboard, October, 1971

"Banks of the Ohio"

Olivia definitely was beginning to feel her own sound emerge with "Banks of the Ohio." The old ballad, made popular by Joan Baez, became transformed under the energies of Olivia and the arrangement expertise of Welch and Farrar.

The song starts simply with a regular beat. But the almost-monotonous 1-2 beat comes alive under the electronic strings. In the first verse of the simple story of unreturned love, only Olivia's voice is heard. Male back-up voices, including that of deep bass singer Mike Sammes, join her on the chorus.

As the second-verse lyrics pick up on the knife scene, Olivia's pitch picks up and the electric guitar stretches higher and tighter. As the balladeer realizes the murderous act in the third verse, an electric piano intensifies the feeling. High female voices and an electronic harmonica come in to add complexity to the final chorus.

What started out as a simple, old-fashioned ballad ended up becoming a rich expression. Olivia's sound was easy and rolling like the plains of Australia, but her sound was also dotted with peaks like the ranges in the distant Melbourne sky. Later, some people would call Olivia's music "country," others would say "pop" and "folk." Whatever the category, Olivia's sound was coming from a woman who knew both city and country.

"Banks of the Ohio" went straight onto the British charts and gave Olivia her first Silver Disc (representing sales in excess of a quarter million dollars). The fans in Australia liked Olivia's version enough so that there she received a Gold Disc (representing a half million dollars in sales). Germany, South Africa and Denmark followed suit.

Toward an Image

Two single hits did not make an instant star of Olivia Newton-John. But Olivia was not one to sit and wait for stardom to come to her.

She spent most of 1971 touring the European continent with Cliff Richard. Olivia also began learning the ropes of song festivals at this time. In most countries, except America, song festivals are major steps in becoming well known. In 1971, Olivia was able to participate in the Antibes Song Festival in Europe. While she didn't win, it gave her confidence and experience.

Though Olivia had done a few recordings, she had the chance to enlarge her experience by recording with Cliff Richard. It was the first time he had ever recorded with a woman — an indication of Richard's opinion of the young Australian singer.

Olivia's voice became better known in 1972 because she had become a regular guest on the BBC-TV series, "It's Cliff Richard." It helped, too, that she racked up another successful single, "What is Life?". While the song became a hit in Britain, it was never released in the United States.

16

Olivia was captivating the English. She was voted the Best British Girl Singer by readers of the pop weekly, *Record Mirror,* in both 1971 and 1972. Olivia enjoyed performing; and people enjoyed Olivia's wide, wholesome smile and the whispering, almost child-like quality in her voice. For Olivia, a high spot of 1972 came when she appeared with French singer Sacha Distel at the grand Prince of Wales Theatre. It was exciting and hectic keeping pace through tours and performances in England. Still, Olivia knew that time was slipping by since she had recorded "If Not For You" and "Banks of the Ohio." Even though Olivia was busy performing, she knew that years without hit recordings are sparse years.

At the end of 1972, Festival Records released a second album, *Olivia.* The album met with moderate success in England as Olivia continued her tour of various countries. She participated in the 1973 Tokyo Song Festival. While Olivia was taking top female awards in England, she was just beginning to receive few, but good, reviews in America.

The well-traveled singer was delighted when she landed a spot on the Dean Martin Show early in 1973. But she hardly saw "Dino." "He doesn't come to rehearsals," she said. "He just comes on when everything is set up. He's so professional."

Though Olivia would not say it, she, too, was quite professional even in those beginning days. She was a world traveler, but she showed none of the show-business glitter that often accompanies that life style. Reviewers were using descriptive phrases such as, "definitely sunny," "wholesome," "good family entertainment" when describing Olivia's performances.

For a beginning singer, any attention from the press seems good. But after some reviews, Olivia began to twinge with uneasiness about her image in England. She wasn't sure the "definitely sunny" image was entirely true. But Olivia went on with her schedule, figuring that perhaps if she forgot about the comments, her genuine image would emerge.

Late in 1973, Olivia's single and her album, *Let Me Be There,* was released in the United States. The country-flavored song immediately inspired rave reviews, even by country-saturated Nashville fans.

This country twist startled Olivia. She was amazed to

see "Let Me Be There" receive widespread country charting and air play, and also fly to the top 10 on the pop charts. A tour of the States to support the single would have to be the next order of business. But before that trip, Olivia decided on a quick trip to Australia to visit her father and her stepmother.

Olivia was in Australia at the beginning of 1974 when she found out that she was chosen to be Britain's representative in that year's Eurovision Song Festival. It was the biggest and most important song festival in Europe. "The phone rang in the middle of the night," Olivia told a reporter, "and there was this reporter on the line from London asking me how I felt to have been chosen. It was the first I knew about it. I felt thrilled and nervous. It was a real honor to represent Britain." The year before, England's favorite superstar, Cliff Richard, had been its representative. He had won easily. The English felt sure that Olivia, too, had the ability to take the prize.

As a participant, Olivia had to sing six songs in the eliminating process during Jimmy Savile's Club Click BBC-1 TV series. The viewers voted for the song which would be the United Kingdom's entry. Olivia felt all the songs except one of high standards. To her disappointment, the viewers chose the song she cared for least — "Long Live Love." Since Olivia could choose what to wear for the competition, she decided on trousers. However, viewers suggested a dress. Since she was representing Britain, Olivia felt obliged to wear what the viewers wanted and sing their choice of song. Though she compromised graciously, Olivia was beginning to feel hemmed in by other people's image of her.

But Olivia had more to think about than the April Eurovision contest. She had made a pilot TV show for BBC in 1973, and the producers had then scheduled her to make four more shows early in 1974. The shows surprised many viewers. They had expected a format with lots of singing and dancing, similar to the style of the Cliff Richard shows. But instead, Olivia gave them songs linked together by poetry. The show was called "Moods of Love," and producer Nick Hunter allowed Olivia to try out many of her own ideas. Olivia was happy with the shows. They satisfied her artistic sense and they also gave her the chance to return some favors. "I was able to have Cliff on my show. I've always been on his, and it was great to have a chance to ask him back."

Olivia also co-starred in a special featurette film with England's Georgia Fame.

Meanwhile, in the States, Olivia's "Let Me Be There" was earning her awards as well as popularity. The Country Music Association named her 1974 female vocalist of the year. She was presented a Grammy award as Best Female Country Vocalist — the first time a British singer had won in Country Music category. Olivia also won the award as the Most Promising Female Vocalist from the Academy of Country Music. She merited all of these citations for a song that "hardly sold a copy" in England!

Olivia was eager to start her tour of the States. But, as a professional, Eurovision would have to come first. The pressure was getting to her. She didn't feel comfortable with the selected song, but she couldn't voice any objection. It was a relief simply to have the contest come so that it would soon be over for her.

The sun came up and went down on April 6, 1974; and it did not see Olivia Newton-John win the Eurovision Song Festival in Brighton.

As a reviewer for *Melody Maker* said shortly after the

contest, "It was nothing short of murderous to hear her fine control and phrasing buried beneath the devouring chomping noise of 'Long Live Love.' " The same reporter decided to question Olivia to discover her feelings about the "baby food image" of her that the English had been served.

"Do I feel that in England I have to be the nice girl-next-door? Yes, slightly. I feel that's what people expect of me because up till now that's the image I've had."

Olivia went on to tell the reporter, "In America my image is completely opposite to what it is here. They think of me quite differently as an artist. I'm able to be more myself. I not only have different songs; but I look different, too." Once Eurovision was over, Olivia felt she could express her frustrations about the certain song and the certain look she had to maintain. The press, however, felt her comments were "sour grapes." They felt she couldn't take the defeat. The *Melody Maker* reporter, however, felt that Olivia emerged from the contest stronger and with a deeper sense of her own identity and potential. "It seems unlikely that Olivia will again allow herself to be propelled into something that she feels does not suit her."

Just after Eurovision, Olivia flew to the United States to begin a six-month tour. While traveling, Olivia remembered the audience's reaction to her first show in America in 1973. "I wore jeans and that was exciting enough. And I thought 'They still clap and I'm wearing jeans,' " Olivia related. She was beginning to realize "in that environment, it's the music they come for; the glamour bit just doesn't come into it." It astounded Olivia that people came just to hear her. Fans in fourteen cities would be waiting for her 1974 tour.

"Let Me Be There"

Olivia's first hit, "If Not For You," was not written as a country song. But Olivia's version of the Dylan piece gave it a definite country feel and prepared American fans for the album, *Let Me Be There.* John Rostill, who wrote the song for Olivia, was very much interested in country music before he died from a suicide-inspired drug overdose in 1973. The lyrics reflect a simple country theme — "Let me change whatever's wrong and make it right."

The steady beat in "Let Me Be There," "If Not For You," and "Banks of the Ohio" contrasts with the kind of soft lilt Olivia gives to "Love Song" on this album. The acoustic and electric guitars give an almost ethereal feel to Olivia's soft echoing voice in "Love Song." Shimmering trinkets heard in the background enhance Olivia's recurring phrasing, "'You know what I mean, have your eyes really seen." The words to "Love Song," though written by Lesley Duncan and recorded by other stars, seem to be made for Olivia's interpretation.

Indeed, Olivia doesn't need songs composed just for her in order to show her talent. John Denver's "Take Me Home Country Roads" did almost as well for Olivia as it did for the songwriter himself. "Have you heard her version?" an enthusiastic Denver asked an interviewer. "The introduction comes on like gangbusters." Olivia's introduction, with electric organ accompaniment, sounds like a full choir.

Olivia smiled when she was told of Denver's compliment. "The beginning was my idea."

The album shows Olivia's vocal variety. "Angel of the Morning" rings with a plaintive quality interspersed with

22

piercing intensity. Her voice is capable of reaching a very high range — audible only to angels it seems sometimes.

Again, the electric guitar backup to "If I Could Read Your Mind" gives Olivia's version a country sound in comparison to Gordon Lightfoot's folk interpretation. That song, and Kris Kristofferson's "Help Me Make It Through the Night," show Olivia's penchant for ballads. Her voice and her sensibility bend easily and agilely around the sung stories. "Just A Little Too Much" shows just how thoroughly a woman with a clipped British-Australian accent can throw herself into a genuine Nashville country sound.

On Tour

Unfortunately for Olivia Newton-John, touring involves flying. On her first brief tour of the United States in 1973, Olivia left the States for England on a Friday, the thirteenth. She felt it was an unlucky start to her trip. Her flight was in the air only an hour when the plane started lurching and the man seated next to her was convinced the plane was crashing. Olivia rushed up to the stewardess to find out what was happening. Since engine trouble had developed, the pilots were jettisoning fuel before returning to New York. Olivia landed safely but she has been fearful of flying ever since.

One thing Olivia is not afraid of is an audience. Or, if she is, she doesn't show it. On the 1974 tour, Olivia found American audiences appreciative and loyal. But when appearances in several cities were cramped into a short time, things became a blur for Olivia. "Every morning when I wake up, I always check the matchbooks near the hotel bed to see where I am," she once said.

Touring means a variety of activities. Olivia does TV specials, hosting *The Midnight Special* one night and appearing on *The Johnny Carson Show* another. She also does concerts in several cities, performs in Las Vegas and has been the drawing attraction at state fairs. During the latter, Olivia usually tries to find time for the rodeo to watch one of her loves — horses.

Las Vegas was indeed a highlight of her 1974 tour. She appeared on the same show as Charlie Rich, another country entertainer. He, too, was appearing there for the first time. Like Olivia, Charlie Rich is also popular on the rock scene with many country hits that have "crossed over" to pop.

Olivia finds that one of the biggest disadvantages of touring is having too much restaurant food. When Olivia was in Dallas, she convinced one of the band players who was from Dallas to take them all home for some real cooking. Olivia, too, even took some time out to prepare a dinner for manager Peter Gormley, and co-producers Bruce Welch and John Farrar and the band. She seemed quite proud of her leg of lamb gourmet meal.

So far, Olivia's favorite American city has been San Francisco. Interestingly, the gandeur of San Francisco is contrasted to the congestion of Los Angeles in the same way that Melbourne was always contrasted to Sydney. San Francisco probably appealed to Olivia because it reminded her of home. At the present, she handles her heavy touring schedule by renting a Malibu beach house in California for six months and retaining an apartment in London for the other six months of the year.

U. S. 1910517

Olivia takes her own band with her to each new city. She thinks there would be too many problems picking up a new group in each city. As with most troubadours, the dash to airport, to hotel, to show site and back to hotel frazzles Olivia. It's no wonder that, even though it's stimulating to see fans, Olivia enjoys recording more than touring. "I think I like recording best because it means I can sing a lot," she has said.

"If You Love Me Let Me Know"

Olivia records in England, using Australian musicians, and singing mostly in a country vein. If there were any doubt about Olivia Newton-John's sound, the album, *If You Love Me,* definitely marks it as a unique country sound.

Olivia seems to have gained more confidence in her ability to select songs that are right for her. Each song on the album rings true. It's done exactly right. The two biggest hits of the album — "If You Love Me Let Me Know" and "I Honestly Love You" — couldn't be more unlike. The latter sails along smoothly like a cumulous cloud; the former moves to a definite upbeat tempo.

"Country Girl" smacks of a young girl striking out on her own. Yet Olivia knows how to show mixed emotions by poignantly avoiding the tear in her mother's eye. All the lyrics roll off Olivia's tongue like honey on country biscuits. The toe-tapping, hand-clapping beat in "The River's Too Wide" affects even the cynic who think bridges of kindness can never be built. For 3 minutes, 16 seconds, listeners are sure that Olivia herself can stretch the bridge across to the other side.

Technically, Olivia's own composition, "Changes," may not be the best song on the album. But it is certainly the most poignant. In her song, she delicately describes the traumatic effects of divorce on a child. The theme is one which holds interest for Olivia. Frequently, when interviewers ask Olivia about her plans to marry her present manager, Lee Kramer, Olivia is reluctant. "My parents, my older sister, and so many of my friends have been divorced. And I'm not ready for children yet." Olivia sings "Changes" as if she knew of what she speaks.

Olivia and the Country

Can Olivia Newton-John really be considered a country singer when she wasn't born in Nashville or raised on the Grand Ole Opry? That is the question which some country singers are raising.

Olivia has answered, "I've never claimed to be a country singer; to call yourself that, you'd have to be born in that background. I simply love country music and its straightforwardness." She compares herself to Mac Davis who sings any style he likes, even opera and to Charlie Rich who began his career as a jazz musician.

"Country has changed from the old, harsh, nasal style," Olivia has also said, "and I think that is why it is being accepted by people from all walks of life. Or maybe the world has just lost some of its snobbishness." Olivia knows where she stands on the issue, and it is clear that critics will not dampen her fresh spirit.

Country music has been through many changes since its beginnings with the first settlers in America. During the 1940's, country music (that is, music of the southeast) began to merge with the more sophisticated music of the west. Hence, country-and-western music. Out of this merging came musicians like Merle Travis, Webb Pierce and Hank Williams. The steel guitar, drums and even horn sections of the western swing bands were borrowed as backups for southeastern vocalists.

Today, the merging in music continues. It isn't as easy to put music and musicians into definite categories. Country music is an eclectic sound — music that draws upon a wide variety of musical sources.

Discussing her own style, Olivia says she started out as a folk singer. "But no one else was singing that sort of country music. It suited me," she has said, "and so I just sort of fell into it." "Country Roads" became her first big country hit in England.

Today, however, her country-type songs aren't as popular in England as they are in the United States. To satisfy the different tastes of the different markets, Olivia records certain albums for the U.S. market and others for the English.

Country music appeals to Olivia because the "melodies are pretty, the songs are nice to sing, the words are great." She resents those who accuse her of putting on a Nashville accent. "I don't put on an American or a Nashville accent. . . . When people sing, they pronounce words in a different way," she says. With singers like Olivia, the close harmonies and the sentimental lyrics of country music are gaining international appeal.

"Have You Never Been Mellow?"

Again, John Farrar came up with another perfect song and arrangement for Olivia — "Have You Never Been Mellow?". Olivia sings it as though she really does know what it's like to be in a hurry and then to discover the why-rush attitude. She sings like one who has discovered strength in some dependence. The song has impact particularly because Olivia is such an independent person. She has struggled through the "other people's image" of her and has come up with her own image — with limitations, of course, — but an image with which she's comfortably mellow.

Actually, the whole album, titled after its hit song, has a mellow quality to it. Most of the songs flow like the rolling river in "Lifestream." Melodic strings are the undercurrent to Olivia's haunting "The Air That I Breathe." She harmonizes with herself on the high lines of the chorus. The song almost casts a spell with its soft magic.

Olivia shows her interest in John Denver's music by using two of his songs on this album, "Goodbye Again," and "Follow Me." However, she does the songs in a version almost identical to Denver's own. She excels in the songs written especially for her. "Please, Mr. Please," by Bruce Welch and John Rostill, is a case in point. The twang of the electric guitar is offset by the piping flute and by the way Olivia softly chants the sad memories a song can bring to mind. The album ends with this song and leaves the listener wanting "to hear that song again."

Image for Tomorrow

Though she never worked the cramped stage of the Grand Ole Opry, Olivia Newton-John took the top female vocalist of the year award at the 1974 Country Music Association's awards in October. Olivia had to be in England when the awards were announced, so she had recorded a film clip of appreciation in case she won. She said on the film that she wanted to visit Nashville and thank them in person for the awards.

Some country singers grumbled at Olivia's awards and set about starting a new country music association. They wanted to award only those who played the Grand Old Opry. Lorretta Lynn, top female country singer, however, said, "I've won four awards in England, and I'm not jealous. . . . I'm happy when somebody else comes along."

1975 started out in the same key. Olivia was named 1975 Rising Star on CBS-TV's recent Entertainer of the Year Awards. From there, things skyrocketed. *People* magazine featured Olivia in the cover story as the "hottest new pipes in pop." She was nominated for four American Music Awards on the ABC-TV special. Olivia walked away with them all — Favorite Pop Single, "I Honestly Love You"; Top Country Album, *Let Me Be There;* and Favorite Female Vocalist in both pop and country categories.

It was no small thing to win the Favorite Female Vocalist, for Olivia competed against Barbra Streisand and Helen Reddy in pop and Loretta Lynn and Marie Osmond in country.

The awards didn't stop, and the year was still new. On March 1, Olivia won the CBS-TV Grammy for Best Pop Performance by a female and the music industry's biggest honor of all — Record of the Year — for "I Honestly Love You." Again, competition was fierce for this last award — Elton John's "Don't Let the Sun Go Down On Me," Roberta Flack's "Feel Like Makin' Love," Joni Mitchell's "Help Me," and Maria Muldaur's "Midnight at the Oasis."

Three days later, on another national CBS-TV special, Olivia, along with Barbra Streisand, was voted as the "People's Choice" for "Best-Loved Female Singer." From

1974 to 1975, Olivia has earned seven gold records and two platinum ones. In 1975, her most recent album, *Have You Never Been Mellow?*, hit number 1 on the national charts.

In May, 1975, Olivia went back to Las Vegas.
"Olivia Newton-John, golden princess, seems to have the unique ability for winning an audience the moment she opens those vocal chords."

The crowd was enthusiastic and overflowing as she skipped on stage, dressed elegantly but simply in a white gown flowing to the floor. She was backed by a full string section as well as her own touring band.
Olivia possesses the sort of charisma and grace that brings to mind the over-used analogy of the girl-next-door.
Olivia's simple, unadorned personality remains constant on and off stage.

When she sings, the material speaks with the same simple forcefulness that is so compelling in her personality.
Cashbox, May 17, 1975

She may look like the girl next door, yet the hit singer is from across the ocean and from the land "down under." She has a sense of ease and peacefulness, not one of glamour and show, as she moves with her music. She may continue to win awards but she will not take on the glitter of superstardom. Olivia is not one geared for overkill. She is just herself, struggling to remain fresh and alive, pure and simple.

JACKSON FIVE   NEIL DIAMOND
CARLY SIMON   CAROLE KING
BOB DYLAN   DIANA ROSS
JOHN DENVER   THE OSMONDS
THE BEATLES   CHARLIE RICH
ELVIS PRESLEY   ELTON JOHN
JOHNNY CASH   CHICAGO
CHARLEY PRIDE   FRANK SINATRA
ARETHA FRANKLIN   BARBRA STREISAND
ROBERTA FLACK   OLIVIA NEWTON-JOHN
STEVIE WONDER

Rock'n PopStars